To the memory of Richard F. Cunningham, my fellow fisherman
—E. M.

For Cindy and Amy Vanderbeek, my third and fourth favorite nieces
—D. V.

Rabbit Ears Books is an imprint of Rabbit Ears Productions, Inc.
Published by Simon & Schuster, Inc.
1230 Avenue of the Americas
New York, New York 10020

Manufactured in the United States of America.
10 9 8 7 6 5 4 3 2 1

Library of Congress Cataloging-in-Publication Data
Metaxas, Eric.
Stormalong / written by Eric Metaxas ; illustrated by Don Vanderbeek.
p. cm.
Summary: Recounts some of the astounding adventures of the legendary New England sea captain
who could tie an octopus in knots.
ISBN 0-689-80194-7
1. Stormalong, Alfred Bulltop—Legends. [1. Stormalong, Alfred Bulltop—Legends.
2. Tall tales. 3. Folklore—United States.]
I. Vanderbeek, Don, ill. II. Title.
PZ8.1.M518St 1995
398.2'0973'01—dc20   94-48132

STORMALONG

Written by **Eric Metaxas**

Illustrated by **Don Vanderbeek**

Rabbit Ears Books

The story of old Stormalong, the famous New England sea captain, is such a powerfully tall tale that in most cases it's usually a good idea to get a stepladder before ye even begin. But that's just the nature of fish stories.

Now, some folks'll tell ye Stormalong was tyin' knots before rope was invented and weighin' anchors before iron was an element. Some folks'll even try and tell ye he was sailin' boats before there were any oceans to speak of.

They'll try and tell ye he was half bluefish, a quarter octopus, two-fifths cod, three-eighths horseshoe crab, four-thirds sandworm, and a half a dozen fried quahogs with a side order of tartar sauce—but most of that stuff is pure seafoam, so keep yer eyes open, now, mateys. Ye been warned.

Now the actual way that Stormalong came into the world is a pretty tall fish story in its own right. It happened during the big hurricane of 1826. That was the one that bent Cape Cod into the fishhook shape it has to this day. That was some blow, all right. Many folks that had a full head of hair lost it, and some folks that had lost theirs got it back, no questions asked.

Anyway, at the height of the storm, an ambitious young wave that didn't feel it was gettin' the recognition it deserved decided to break away from the pack and head inland. Well, the wave took off down Front Street, then up First, then down Second, and just as though it knew where it was goin' it paused to get its bearings, reared back like a sea horse, crested, then broke into the Widow Stormalong's parlor with a mighty crash, depositing its squalling human flotsam, which is to say our hero, into the middle of the room in the biggest heap of barnacles and seaweed ye ever seen.

The soggy woman was so taken with the sea-born child that she immediately adopted him and decided to name him Alfred Bulltop, after her twin sister, who was a very mean old woman, probably on account of her funny name.

About the only thing that everyone will agree on when the subject of Stormy comes up is that he grew faster than anything they'd ever seen. That boy grew when he was sleepin' and he grew when he was awake. He even managed to grow in between the two some way or another. Man-alive, he was something else.

In time, the salty lad could croak just like a sea robin and was fluent in several of the North Atlantic mackerel tongues. He could even speak a little conversational flounder. And although he never did understand their particular dialect, he was downright chummy with the local shellfish population.

By the time he was ten years old, Stormy got to be such a good sailor that there wasn't a thing on the planet he couldn't tie in knots, and that included rocks and icicles. And, as many a sailor can attest, there wasn't a body of water that was too shallow for him. Why, once after a light rain shower there was just the tiniest bit of dew on the grass. Well, a bunch of kids were skippin' home from the old schoolhouse and there was Stormy tackin' past his mean Aunt Alfred's petunia bed in a dinghy, just as easy as you please.

Now, by the time he was about sixteen, Stormalong decided to seek his fortune on the sea. And so he packed his gear inside a friendly Nantasket octopus, tied the soggy critter onto an oar, and headed north toward Boston. This was during the Golden Era of Sail, mind you, of clipper ships and tall masts.

A gentleman by the name of Donald McKay was buildin' the biggest boats anyone had ever seen. The biggest one of 'em all was a moonraker called the *Widow's Peak*. Stormy knew she was the boat for him and signed up for the next passage.

Now the captain of the *Widow's Peak* was called "Cap'n" for short, but his full name was Captain Phineas Elijah Jeremiah Ebeneezer Josiah Cheever Gesundheit. *(Thank you.)* The galley cook was called Billy Pegleg for short, but his full name was Billy Pegleg, which made it mighty easy to remember. Billy's menu featured the standard seagoin' fare of the day, including such dishes as dandy funk and plum duff, not to mention the most crustaceous lobscouse ye ever pronounced. And Stormy ate it all—and he ate his soup so fast he had to use a spoon with holes in it, just to give the soup a fair shake!

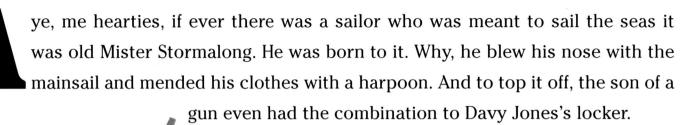

Aye, me hearties, if ever there was a sailor who was meant to sail the seas it was old Mister Stormalong. He was born to it. Why, he blew his nose with the mainsail and mended his clothes with a harpoon. And to top it off, the son of a gun even had the combination to Davy Jones's locker.

Aye, that was the life for Stormy, and he knew it. In the evenings he'd lay out on the foredeck and look at the shootin' stars, and you could hear him singing sea chanteys that were so touchin' the barnacles would cry:

"Oh, the Cape Cod girls they have no combs,
they comb their hair with codfish bones.
Cape Cod boys they have no sleds, they
slide down dunes on codfish heads.
Cape Cod doctors they have no pills, they
give their patients codfish gills."

Aye, those were halcyon days, all right. But things weren't always peaceful. . . .

Now every lad and lassie has heard fearsome tales of horrible sea monsters twice as long as clipper ships, who roam the briny deep jest awaitin' to wrap their slimy coils around whatever unlucky vessel should happen to pass and drag it to a watery grave.

Well, one time we came upon a wrigglin' monster of the deep such as no man has ever laid his peepers on and lived to tell the tale! It had two hundred coils if it had twenty and its mouth had two dozen sets of the most jagged snaggle-teeth ye ever saw. When the bos'n spied him in his glass he gave out a shriek like a schoolgirl, "Aahhh!" and dove into the ship's hold and so did everyone else. Everyone but Stormalong, that is. The very moment he saw the monster he got a gleam in his eye, and before you could say, "Columbus, Ohio," he'd leapt off the bowsprit like it was a divin' board.

Aye, that was a fearsome battle. The two of 'em wrestled around for the longest time, and then suddenly they disappeared. The water got as smooth as glass and we began to wonder if he'd ever surface again. But Stormy could hold his breath for some time, three weeks to be exact. Still, though, after three weeks there was no sign of him and we gave him up for dead. It was mighty sad.

Well, there we were, all ready to weigh anchor and set sail. Then shiver me timbers if he and that tangled-up sea critter didn't pop out of the water like a couple of giant lobster floats. And they were still goin' at it, tooth and tentacle, tentacle and tooth, tooth and tentacle. Well, it was over soon after that, and by the time Stormalong was through with that stretched-out serpent, he'd tied so many different kinds of knots in it that it just up and contradicted itself to death!

Well, by this time Stormy had reached adulthood, but that didn't stop him from growin'. He got so big it just took our breath away. And he ate so much that we had to serve him his shark's soup out of a wooden dinghy. In time, Stormalong got so darn big that even the *Widow's Peak* herself wasn't big enough for him. Things got so tight that one night the poor feller rolled over in his sleep and fell overboard.

"That tears it!" he said, with tears in his eyes. "I'm swallowin' the anchor!"—which was sailor for *I quit!* "Next time we dock I'm headin' inland."

I could see his heart was broken over it, but Stormy said he was just goin' to put an oar over his shoulder and keep walking until he was so far from the ocean that no one would have the slightest idea what an ocean was, and that would be just far enough.

It was the worst day of his life, but Stormalong did like he said and took his oar and his octopus and started inland.

He walked roughly two thousand miles west when round about Utah he met a man by the roadside. "Do you know what this is?" he asked the man, indicating the oar.

"No, I don't. And I don't care neither. I'll tell you this, though, you'd better get that jackrabbit of yours looked at. It may be none of my business, but all the same it seems to me that little feller needs a little medical attention. That's what I think. You asked me and I'm tellin' ya."

Well, you couldn't get farther inland than that, so Stormy got himself a piece of land and began farmin'. But it wasn't long before the pull of the old saltwater got to him. Stormy just sat down in his tomato patch and started squallin' like a newborn babe. I reckon he just got seasick for his old friends.

Then the salt in his tears reminded him of the ocean, which only made him cry harder, and the more he cried, the sadder he got, until he'd cried the entire Great Salt Lake into existence.

Anyway, by the time Stormy got back to Boston things had changed. The Golden Age of Sail was comin' to the end of its passage. Ye see, steamships had come onto the scene. But when Stormy heard about 'em, he just couldn't believe his ears.

"A ship without sails!" he shouted. "Without so much as a leeward or a windward!"

Well, it made about as much sense to him as a jellyfish without jelly. Stormy knew he'd never sail one of 'em.

But Donald McKay knew Stormalong would come back to the sea someday and he'd been preparin' for the occasion by building the largest clipper ship there ever was. It was the sailin' ship to end all sailin' ships. It was called the *Courser*, and nothin' like it ever sailed the seven seas.

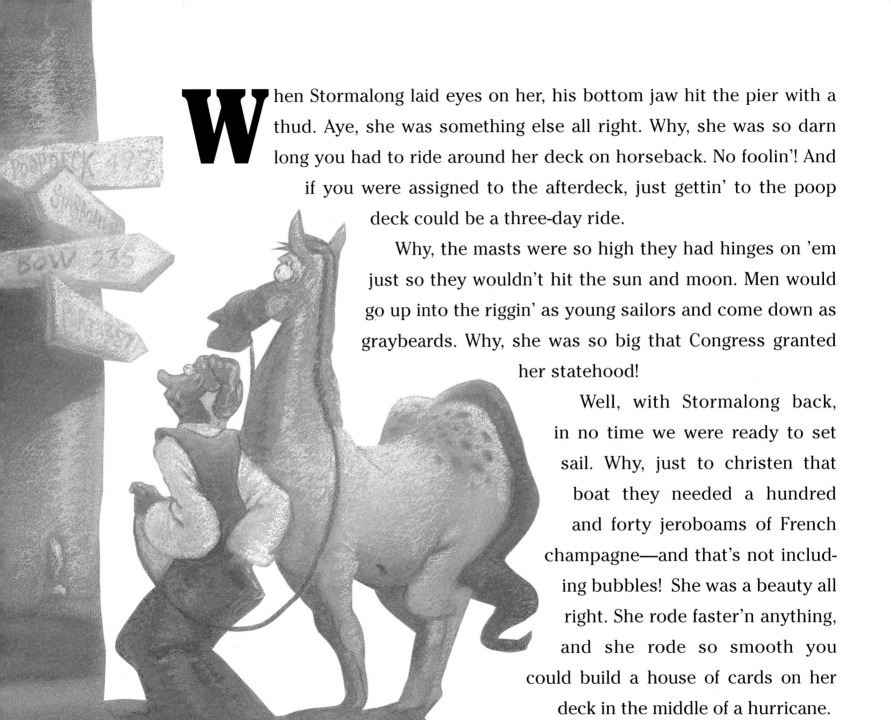

When Stormalong laid eyes on her, his bottom jaw hit the pier with a thud. Aye, she was something else all right. Why, she was so darn long you had to ride around her deck on horseback. No foolin'! And if you were assigned to the afterdeck, just gettin' to the poop deck could be a three-day ride.

Why, the masts were so high they had hinges on 'em just so they wouldn't hit the sun and moon. Men would go up into the riggin' as young sailors and come down as graybeards. Why, she was so big that Congress granted her statehood!

Well, with Stormalong back, in no time we were ready to set sail. Why, just to christen that boat they needed a hundred and forty jeroboams of French champagne—and that's not including bubbles! She was a beauty all right. She rode faster'n anything, and she rode so smooth you could build a house of cards on her deck in the middle of a hurricane.

One time we had to go through the English Channel, but the *Courser* was so darn broad in the beam we didn't know if she'd make it through. Stormalong sent every hand overboard in bos'n's chairs, and he made us soap up the starboard side. Well, we squeaked through all right, but without the soap we would've been stuck for sure. Most of the soap got scraped off around about Dover, and if you ever go there you'll see that the cliffs are as white as they were that very day.

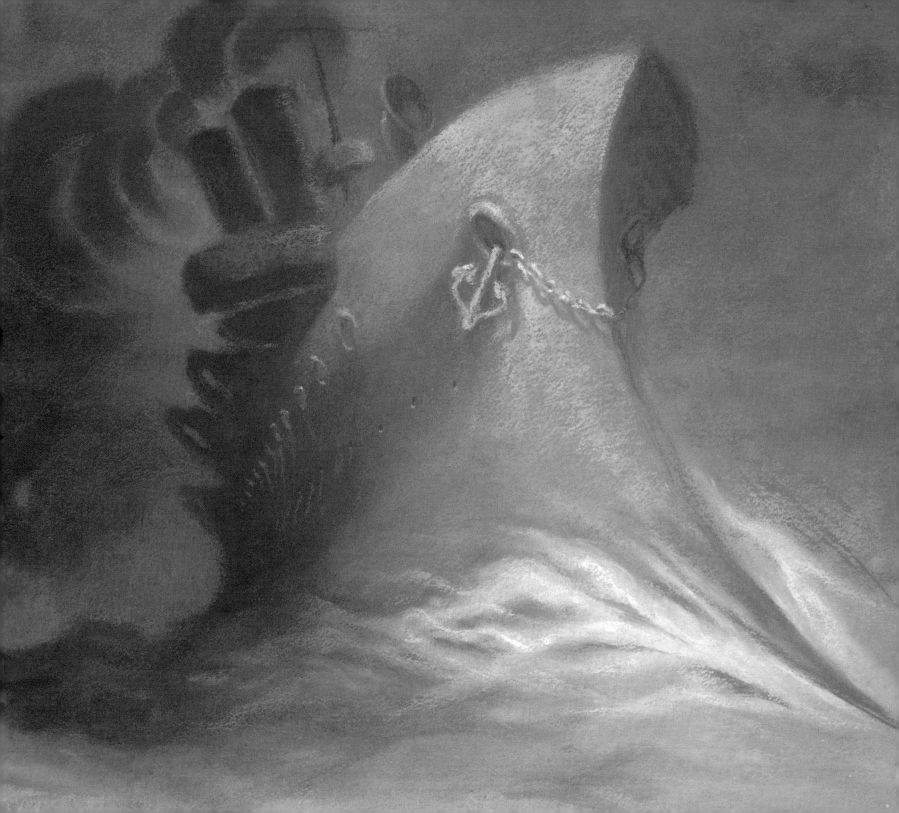

Well, Stormalong was in his glory again. But it wasn't very long before we spotted the *Liverpool Packet*, a huge, powerful steamship that out-steamed all the others. We were roundin' Cape Horn at the time. The captain of the *Packet* had heard about Stormy and the *Courser,* and as soon as they got within hailin' distance they challenged us to a race, from Cape Horn right up to Boston. Well, that got Stormy's ire up like nothing ever had. He'd never let an iron ship defeat a wooden sailin' ship.

"Avast there, mateys, and lay to!" he shouted.

Well, the race started, and we were pretty near even up until we hit the equator.

Ye see, they were just about completing work on the equator at the time, and old Stormalong decided to give 'em a hand with it. Ye see, they'd miscalculated their measurements, and it turned out to be a knot too short.

"A knot too short!" said Stormalong with a wink. "Well, just leave it to me. Knots is me specialty."

With that, Stormalong tied one end of the equator to the foremast, ran all the way to the stern, leaned over, and grabbed the other end of the equator, which was just lyin' there in the water—equators float, ye know—and he pulled and he pulled with all his might until the two ends met. Then, in a flash of inspiration, he invented a new knot that he called a super-equatorial-double-triple-trailer hitch with a peppermint twist. And that was that.

He threw the equator overboard and we were on our way. The knot's still there, by the way, but you'll only see it on higher quality maps.

And now, back to the race. . .

Well, we were far behind, but the wind had picked up something fierce. We stretched every piece of canvas that was available, but it didn't look good. Then, Stormy got an idea.

"Take yer clothes off, ye scalawags," he said. "There's enough wind for every stitch we've got!"

Well, we did what he said and then we really began to make up some lost ground. But it still looked like we weren't goin' to make it in time to beat the steamer to Bean Town.

So then Stormy told us all to shed our skivvies. "Now blow yer lungs dry, mateys," he shouted. "Blow for all yer worth!"

And blow we did, because none of us could bear the thought of losin' to a steamship. Well, there we were, as naked as jaybirds and a-huffin' and puffin' like there was no tomorrow. I don't think the crew of the *Packet* knew what they were lookin' at, but inch by inch we pulled up along side of 'em.

T hen, in a burst of inspiration and expiration, too, Stormy himself shed his own skivvies, strung 'em up, took a deep five-fathom breath and blew a tornado's worth of wind. It sounded like an angry foghorn. Well, that was all it took. We flew by that sorry steamship like it was draggin' ten mud hooks.

When we pulled into the Boston harbor we were a full half a knot ahead of the *Packet* and every deepwater sailor that ever lived was out on the docks a-cheerin' us home.

"Hooray for Stormalong!" they shouted. "Hooray for all the iron men in all the wooden ships! *Hooray!*"

Aye, it was enough to make the hardest shellback weep with abandon.

Well, that was the last passage of the old *Courser*, but Stormy wasn't done with sailin' that easy. One day, around 1910, he just grabbed the tail of Halley's Comet and hitched a ride into outer space. In fact, he's up there yet, sailing from galaxy to galaxy, drinkin' out'a the Big Dipper, harpoonin' Pisces, and jugglin' the moons of Neptune.

I saw him just last week, through a neighbor's telescope. He's bigger than ever now. He says hello to all of you and asks if you could tell the Widow Stormalong hello the next time you see her. Ye see, she ain't heard from him in almost two hundred years now and she's something of a worrier. And don't forget dear Aunt Alfred. She's got feelings, too, ye know. Well, so long, mateys!